wh▽opie!

wh opie pies

whoopie pies

Dozens of Mix 'em, Match 'em, Eat 'em Up Recipes

by **Sarah Billingsley and Amy Treadwell**

Photographs by **Antonis Achilleos**

CHRONICLE BOOKS
SAN FRANCISCO

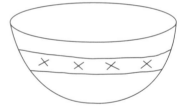

Library of Congress Cataloging-in-Publication Data is available.

ISBN 978-0-8118-7454-0

Manufactured in China.

Design by vanessa dina
Illustrations by vanessa dina
Prop styling by spork
Food styling by cristina besher
Photo background patterns by repot depot
Typesetting by janis reed

10 9 8 7 6 5 4 3

Chronicle Books LLC
680 Second Street
San Francisco, CA 94107
www.chroniclebooks.com

dedication

Dedicated to Pennsylvania and Massachusetts, where we ate our first whoopie pies (ahem, gobs!) and became smitten. Let our obsession be your obsession.

acknowledgments

Thanks to:

Amy's daughter, Maxine, who selflessly taste-tested every whoopie pie we baked.

Kevin Townsend, for mining his childhood memories so we could re-create the classic marshmallow cream filling. We hope it lives up to his high expectations.

Joel Rosenblatt, who declared whoopie pies "junk" but nevertheless encouraged this pastry project when it took over both his kitchen and his woman.

Ron and Karen Billingsley, for encouraging all childhood baking experiments, even chocolate chip omelets.

A major shout-out to all the supporters and tasters at Chronicle Books: You flocked from every corner of the building. We are all a bit fatter and merrier now.

makin' whoopie!

the cakes

the creamy fillings

makin' whoopie!

Introduction

What is a whoopie pie?

For those living in the Northeast (for our purposes, roughly from Pennsylvania to Maine), the whoopie pie (or gob) is a familiar treat. Not quite a sandwich cookie, not quite a cake, whoopie pies are marked by two characteristics: their soft, rounded shape and a generous amount of creamy filling. If your treat is flat or thinly filled, we're sorry to say that it's not a proper whoopie pie.

The origin of both the name and the treat are murky (though we offer some theories throughout this book). What we do know is that the "classic" and overall favorite variety of whoopie pie is chocolate cake with marshmallow filling. This is the whoopie most likely to be found next to cash registers at mom-and-pop shops, gas stations, and diners throughout the region, wrapped tightly in plastic wrap. (Eating the moist whoopie "skin" stuck to the plastic is a unique pleasure, especially if your mom makes you share your whoopie pie with your brother or sister.) Flavors such as vanilla, chocolate chip, and especially pumpkin are also common.

Who are these authors?

Amy honed her whoopie tasting skills while growing up in Massachusetts. In her small hometown south of Boston, whoopies were featured at every school bake sale, and she was always first in line to buy one. And since her mother didn't make whoopie pies at home (Amy's mom is a wonderful baker; she's just not a whoopie pie baker), Amy ruthlessly tried to befriend anyone in the neighborhood with a mom who did. As an adult, she has found them in such diverse locations as a little grocery store in Belgrade Lakes, Maine, an Arco gas station just off the interstate highway in New Hampshire, and an old-fashioned country store on Cape Cod.

Sarah explored traditional gob territory across Pennsylvania, from farm-flat Lancaster to the mountainous Laurel Highlands and Blue Knob Ski Resort, near Johnstown. Despite Pittsburghers' affection for gut-busting sandwiches, gobs are not common in this corner of the state (Pittsburgh loves its dainty Polish and Italian cookies). Nevertheless, Sarah discovered a recipe in a tattered, spiral-bound church-lady cookbook and began baking them regularly.

What is this book?

In *Whoopie Pies*, we recreated the classic whoopie pie, with its dark chocolaty cake and creamy marshmallow filling. And we also included its counterpart — luscious vanilla with a rich chocolate buttercream filling. We let our imaginations run wild and came up with great flavor combinations like banana with salty peanut butter filling; pistachio-cardamom with rosewater buttercream; oatmeal with maple filling; even jalapeno-cornbread with bacon-chive goat cheese filling. In fact, we got so caught up in the nearly endless combinations that we organized the recipes in two sections: The Cakes and The Creamy Fillings. We want you to mix and match, so we've given you a nice, long list of possible cake and filling combinations to get you started. The real fun is in mixing and matching the flavors yourselves. Coconut cream filling in a lemon whoopie? Why the heck not?

Our hope is that you learn what we did long ago: Once you go whoopie, you'll never go back.

We both ended up living in San Francisco, a food lover's paradise, but one distinctly devoid of whoopie pies/gobs. As cookbook editors (and enthusiastic home bakers), it seemed almost inevitable that we would not only rhapsodize about these treats of our youth but also come to the conclusion that we should write an entire cookbook on the subject. (And refer to them throughout as whoopie pies, which we both agree is the cuter name.)

Before you start making whoopies:

We are pretty lazy bakers. Sure, we instruct the reader to sift the flour and other dry ingredients, but if you don't, it won't matter too much. We also have other bad baking habits, like reusing our parchment paper and eyeballing measurements for vanilla and lemon zest. Nothing bad has happened to us yet. Rest assured, as long as you keep an eye on the cakes while they're in the oven and have a little fun, you're guaranteed a pretty wonderful whoopie pie.

Whoopie make-ahead

The "cake" component of the whoopie pies can be baked in advance and frozen. Simply bake the cakes as instructed in the recipe, cool them completely, and transfer them to a cookie sheet. Put the cookie sheet with the cakes in the freezer for 1 hour, at which point the cakes will be frozen enough to be stored in a resealable plastic freezer bag without sticking. You can store them in the freezer for up to 1 month.

Most buttercream, ganache, and cream cheese fillings can be made ahead and stored in a covered container in the refrigerator for up to 1 week. Classic Marshmallow and Whipped Chocolate Ganache fillings do not store well and are best used the same day.

When you are ready to assemble the whoopie pies (page 41), remove the cakes from the freezer and defrost at room temperature for at least 2 hours before filling. Remove the creamy fillings from the refrigerator and bring to room temperature about 1 hour before using.

Storage

Whoopie pies are best eaten within a day of making them because they can be a challenge to store. They tend to stick to each other when stacked, so if you need to store them for a few days, find a wide, shallow container so they can be arranged in one layer. If stacking is your only option, that's okay. Just be sure to put a sheet of waxed paper between layers and don't crowd too many together.

You can also wrap whoopies individually in plastic wrap. This method is common in New England, where you'll find individually wrapped whoopies at convenience stores across the region. The outside layer of the cake often sticks to the plastic, but that's part of the charm.

The assembled pies can be stored in an airtight container for up to 3 days.

You'll probably find that storage won't be an issue—they'll all be eaten!

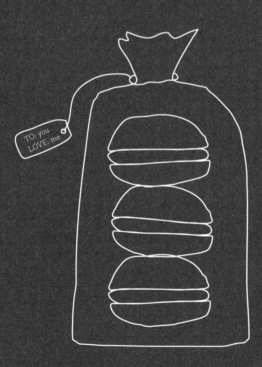

Freezing whoopies whole

Many whoopie pie devotees like to maintain a frozen stash. You can freeze all of the
assembled whoopies pies in this book for up to 1 month (beyond this, most cakes get
mushy and fillings start to taste grainy). It's best to individually wrap and freeze your
whoopie pies. After you have assembled your whoopie pies, transfer them to a cookie
sheet. Freeze for 1 hour, until they are solid. Place into individual small resealable bags.
Zip the bag three-quarters of the way closed, put your lips to the open seam, suck out
the air, and return to the freezer.

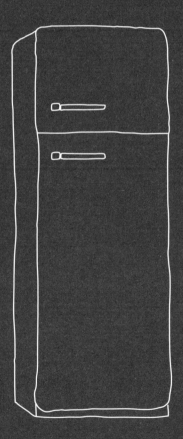

Butter vs. Crisco

No end of experimentation has taught us that, in many cases, vegetable shortening (such as Crisco) is a necessary ingredient to achieve lift, lightness, and that classic rounded whoopie shape. It is also a crucial component of the Classic Marshmallow filling, which will be familiar to anyone from traditional whoopie pie states such as Maine and Pennsylvania.

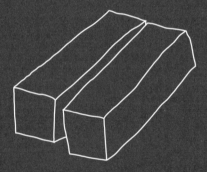

vs.

Filling fluffiness

In most cases, when it comes to making the fillings in this cookbook, the longer you beat the ingredients, the lighter and fluffier the filling. Amy has been known to start up the mixer, leave the room, and forget all about it, but she hasn't wrecked a filling yet.

Whoopies for a crowd

Whoopie pies are real crowd-pleasers, but unless you have access to an industrial kitchen or acres of counter space, baking enough for your family reunion or the entire high school football team can be a real pain. We don't recommend doubling or tripling these recipes; the proportions start to get a bit wonky. Instead, call up a few friends with standing mixers and make as many separate batches as you need. Call it a Whoopie Party, and it's fun for everyone!

Whoopie pie sizing chart

Unless otherwise specified, each recipe will yield enough batter to make:

48 two-inch cakes, for a total of 24 finished whoopie pies (use about 1 tablespoon batter for each cake)

30 four-inch cakes, for a total of 15 finished whoopie pies (use about 2 tablespoons batter for each cake)

If making a cake-size whoopie, you'll get one 9-inch finished pie.

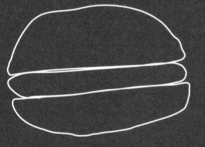

2-inch whoopie pie
(actual size)

4-inch whoopie pie
(actual size)

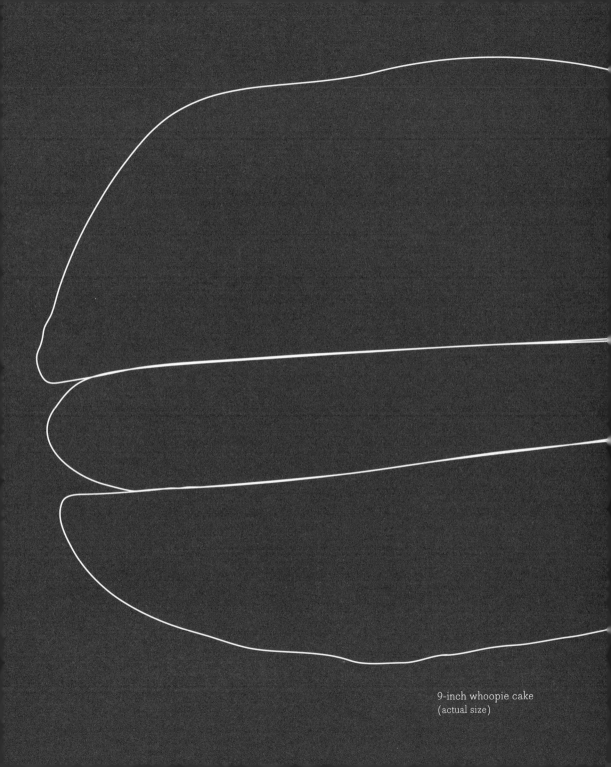

9-inch whoopie cake
(actual size)

Equipment

You don't need fancy equipment to make whoopie pies.
Here are a few items that we've found really useful:

Stand mixer (but you can always
mix whoopies with a hand mixer
or a wooden spoon)

Baking sheets

Two-tablespoon scoop—for the
perfect 4-inch whoopie

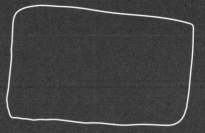

Silpat or other silicone
baking sheet liner

Parchment paper

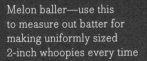

Melon baller—use this
to measure out batter for
making uniformly sized
2-inch whoopies every time

Resealable plastic bags/pastry bags—
use these to fill whoopie pies quickly
and create perfectly round whoopies for
a finished, elegant look

Whoopie fun facts

FACT No. 1
A Whoopie by any other
name would smell as
sweet . . .
    scooter pies
    chocolate drops
    round dogs
    cream cakes
    gobs
    moon pies
    black moons

FACT No. 2
In Bath, Maine, during the Heritage Days festival,
the town holds a whoopie-pie-eating contest.

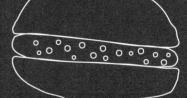

FACT No. 3

Five-hundred people attended the first annual
Whoopie Pie Festival in Dover-Foxcroft, Maine.
One of the judges at the event is now working to
make whoopie pies the state's official dessert.

FACT No. 4

A folklorist and archivist with the South-
western Pennsylvania Heritage Preserva-
tion Commission says the origins of the
whoopie pie are in medieval Germany,
where a cream-filled cake was baked.
German religious groups (such as the
Amish, the Mennonites, and the German
Brethren) that settled in Pennsylvania as
early as 1730 brought the confection.

FACT No. 5

Why "gobs"?

"Gob" is a name owned by Tim Yost of Yost's Dutch Maid Bakery in Johnstown, Pennsylvania, though the name is used widely throughout western Pennsylvania.

Why "gob"? Could be that the miners who carried gobs in their lunch boxes likened them to lumps of coal, which were also called gobs.

FACT No. 6

Why "whoopie"?

The lore is that these were popular treats packed in the lunch boxes of Amish schoolchildren (makes sense, as a frosting sandwich is less messy than frosting on top of a cake). They would pop open their lunch boxes, spot the treat, and shout, "Whoopie!"

FACT No. 7

In 2002, Ben & Jerry's created a "Makin' Whoopie Pie" ice cream flavor. Alas, they have discontinued this important taste sensation, but if you go to www.benjerry.com/contact-us/resurrect.cfm, you can ask Ben and Jerry to reissue it. Let's bring it back, people!

FACT No. 8

Marshmallow Fluff is the main ingredient in the filling of a traditional whoopie pie. Manufactured by the Durkee-Mower Company in Massachusetts (and hard to find for us West Coasters!), Marshmallow Fluff is also an integral part of the famous "Fluffernutter" sandwich—peanut butter and Marshmallow Fluff sandwiched between two pieces of white bread.

Whoopie mix and match

We've organized this book in two major sections: (1) The Cakes, and (2) The Creamy Fillings. Need a little help matching cake with filling? Start out by trying one (or more!) of the following whoopie combinations. The matchups are nearly endless. In fact, we'd love to hear about your own creative combinations. Go to www.chroniclebooks.com and tell us all about your delicious discoveries and also your fabulous disasters.

The Purist

The Classic Chocolate Whoopie (page 43)

Classic Marshmallow (page 76)

Peach Melba

Vanilla Whoopie (page 46)

Raspberry jam or fresh raspberries

Peachy Marshmallow Cream filling (page 100)

Top with a fresh raspberry

Crazy Mo-Fo

Classic Chocolate Whoopie (page 43)

Whipped Chocolate Ganache filling (page 83)

Black and White

½ recipe Vanilla Whoopie (page 46)

½ recipe Classic Chocolate Whoopie (page 43)

Classic Marshmallow filling (page 76)

Use 1 chocolate and 1 vanilla cake for each cookie. Dip half of the assembled whoopie pies in Chocolate Glaze (page 108)

Lemon Flick

Lemon Whoopie (page 52)

Lemon Mascarpone filling (page 97)

Roll edges in crushed lemon candies

The Happy Pilgrim

Pumpkin Whoopie (page 62)

Maple filling (page 93)

Fat Elvis

Banana Whoopie (page 55)

Salty Peanut Butter filling (page 87)

Roll edges in crisped, crumbled bacon

Bee's Knees

Marbled Whoopie (page 49)

Honey Buttercream filling (page 85)

Roll edges in chocolate sprinkles (jimmies)

Lemon Fudgicle

Classic Chocolate Whoopie (page 43)

Lemon curd

Chocolate Ganache filling (page 82)

Lemon Triple Threat

Lemon Whoopie (page 52)

Lemon curd

Lemon Mascarpone filling (page 97)

Root Beer Float

Vanilla Whoopie (page 46)

Root Beer filling (page 95)

Classic Marshmallow filling (page 76)

S'mores

Graham Cracker Whoopie (page 58)

Chocolate Ganache filling (page 82)

Classic Marshmallow filling (page 76)

Hot Cocoa

Classic Chocolate Whoopie (page 43)

Classic Marshmallow filling (page 76)

Chocolate Ganache filling (page 82) for decadence

Dust with cocoa powder

Mochaccino

Mocha Whoopie (page 48)

Whipped Chocolate Ganache filling (page 83)

Classic Buttercream filling (page 81)

Mexican Chocolate

Classic Chocolate Whoopie (page 43)

Chocolate Ganache filling (page 82) mixed with ⅛ teaspoon chili powder and ½ teaspoon ground cinnamon

Roll edges in crushed cocoa nibs

German Chocolate

Classic Chocolate Whoopie (page 43)

Coconut Cream filling (page 88)

Roll edges in toasted coconut and chopped pecans

Death by Chocolate

Classic Chocolate Whoopie (page 43)

Chocolate Buttercream filling (page 79)

Dip in Chocolate Glaze (page 108)

Roll edges in miniature chocolate chips or dark chocolate shavings, optional

Whoopie Satay

Peanut Butter Whoopie (page 54)

Salty Peanut Butter filling (page 87) mixed with ½ teaspoon curry powder

Chocolate Ganache filling (page 82), optional

Dust with confectioners' sugar spiked with curry powder

The Grover

Vanilla Whoopie (page 46)

Classic Buttercream filling (page 81) mixed with ½ ounce blue food coloring

Dust with blue Pixy Stix powdered candy

Stiff Upper Lip

Vanilla Whoopie (page 46)

Chocolate Buttercream filling (page 79)

Roll edges in crushed English toffee candy (such as Heath Bar)

Almond Joyous

Classic Chocolate Whoopie (page 43)

Coconut Cream filling (page 88)

Roll edges in sliced almonds

Hansel (or Gretel)

Gingerbread Whoopie (page 53)

Classic Buttercream filling (page 81)

Create kids faces on tops using extra filling,
a pastry bag, and small, round decorating tip

Candy Striper

Classic Chocolate Whoopie (page 43)

Mint Buttercream filling (page 84)

Roll edges in crushed peppermint candies

Tiramisù

Marbled Whoopie (page 49)

Tiramisù Cream filling (page 98)

Salted Caramel slather (page 90)

Dust edges with cocoa powder

Brisk Morning Constitutional

Oatmeal Whoopie (page 61)

Maple-Bacon filling (page 94)

Rock the Casbah

Pistachio-Cardamom Whoopie (page 57)

Rosewater Buttercream filling (page 86)

Creamsicle

Vanilla Whoopie (page 46)

Orange Cream Cheese filling (page 96)

Orange marmalade

Whoop-er

Classic Chocolate Whoopie (page 43)

Malted Buttercream filling (page 89)

Roll edges in crushed malted milk balls
(such as Whoppers)

My Bloody Valentine

Red Velvet Whoopie (page 44)

Cherry pie filling

Classic Cream Cheese filling (page 80)

Cinnamonylicious

Red Velvet Whoopie (page 44)

Classic Buttercream filling (page 81) mixed
with ½ teaspoon ground cinnamon

Roll edges in cinnamon-flavored candies
(such as Red Hots)

The Stoner

Whoopie Cake (page 71)

Classic Marshmallow filling (page 76)

Drizzle top with Hershey's Chocolate Syrup

Roll edges in crushed Fritos

Serves 1

Argentina, Mama

Vanilla Whoopie (page 46)

Dulce de Leche filling (page 92)

Dust with confectioners' sugar

Guiltless Whoopie

Gluten-Free Chocolate Whoopie (page 68) or Gluten-Free Vanilla Whoopie (page 69)

Vegan Chocolate "Butter" Cream filling (page 105) or Vegan Vanilla "Butter" Cream filling (page 106)

Chipwich

Chocolate Chip Whoopie (page 50)

Classic Marshmallow filling (page 76)

Roll edges in mini chocolate chips

Freeze (optional)

Chip 'n' Dale

Chocolate Chip Whoopie (page 50)

Salty Peanut Butter filling (page 87)

Roll edges in crushed nuts of choice

Mojito

Lemon Whoopie (page 52), using lime instead of lemon

Mint Buttercream filling (page 84)

Piña Colada

Lemon Whoopie (page 52)

Coconut Cream filling (page 88)

Drained crushed pineapple

Garnish with a maraschino cherry

Besame Mucho

Classic Chocolate Whoopie (page 43)

Chocolate Buttercream filling (page 79)

Nutella hazelnut spread

Roll edges in chopped hazelnuts

Dust with cocoa powder

Honey Bun

Jalapeño Cornbread Whoopie (page 73), made without jalapeños

Honey Buttercream filling (page 85)

Incongruous

Carrot Cake Whoopie (page 64)

Root Beer filling (page 95)

Dip in Chocolate Glaze (page 108)

Roll edges in candied shredded carrot

Viennese

Pistachio-Cardamom Whoopie (page 57), replacing pistachios with hazelnuts, and cardamom with ground cinnamon

Classic Buttercream filling (page 81) with raspberries mixed in

Dust with cocoa powder

Fluffernutter

Vanilla Whoopie (page 46)

Salty Peanut Butter filling (page 87)

Marshmallow Fluff

Masked Ginger

Gingerbread Whoopie (page 53)

Candied Ginger filling (page 91)

Chocolate Glaze (page 108)

Fun decorating ideas!

Given the loose definition of a whoopie pie, you can jazz it up any way you wish. Here are some suggestions to get you started:

Spread!

on the inside, in addition to the filling:

Chocolate Ganache (page 82)

Jam

Peanut butter

Whipped cream

Cherry pie filling (or your favorite flavor)

Nutella

Apple butter

Chutney

Pile!

between the cake layers:

Blueberries

Raspberries

Sliced strawberries or bananas

Apples or kiwis, sliced or cut into small pieces

Canned peaches

Chopped nuts

Pudding (any flavor)

Chocolate mousse

Glacé (candied) fruit

Marzipan

Roll!

the edges in:

Miniature chocolate chips

Crushed malted milk balls

Crushed nuts of any kind (pistachios are especially pretty!)

Crushed peppermint candies

Rainbow or chocolate jimmies (sprinkles)

Crushed root beer barrel candies

Red Hots

Crushed toffee candy (such as Heath Bar)

Chopped candied ginger or candied citrus peel

Nonpareils

Dip!

the assembled whoopie pies in:

Chocolate Glaze (page 108)

Lemon glaze

Maple glaze

Vanilla glaze

Melted white chocolate

Warmed peanut butter

Warmed caramel

Candy coating

Glass of milk

Sprinkle!

over the tops of the whoopie pies:

Cocoa powder

Confectioners' sugar

Ovaltine

Ground cinnamon

Grated nutmeg

Five-spice powder

Coarse sea salt

Sesame seeds

Poppy seeds

Candied violets

Cracked black pepper

Pixy Stix powder

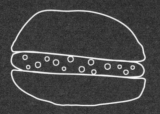

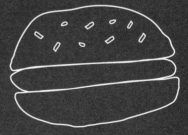

Assembling whoopie pies:

Spread filling onto the flat side of one cake using a knife or spoon.

Top it with another cake, flat-side down.

Repeat with the rest of the cakes and filling.

Alternatively, you can use a pastry bag with a round tip to pipe the filling onto the cakes, which will give you a smoother, neater presentation.

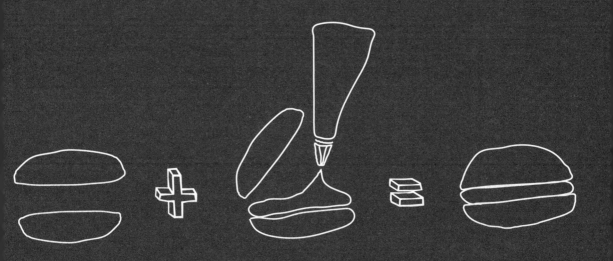

classic chocolate whoopie

Position a rack in the center of the oven and preheat the oven to 375°F. Line two baking sheets with parchment paper.

Sift together the flour, cocoa powder, baking soda, and salt onto a sheet of waxed paper. In the work bowl of a stand mixer fitted with the paddle attachment, beat together the butter, shortening, and brown sugar on low speed until just combined. Increase the speed to medium and beat until fluffy and smooth, about 3 minutes. Add the egg and vanilla and beat for another 2 minutes.

Add half of the flour mixture and half of the milk to the batter and beat on low until just incorporated. Scrape down the sides of the bowl. Add the remaining flour mixture and ½ cup milk and beat until completely combined.

Using a spoon, drop about 1 tablespoon of batter onto one of the prepared baking sheets and repeat, spacing them at least 2 inches apart. Bake one sheet at a time for about 10 minutes each, or until the pies spring back when pressed gently. Remove from the oven and let the cakes cool on the sheet for about 5 minutes before transferring them to a rack to cool completely.

Makes about 48 two-inch cakes.

1⅔ cups all-purpose flour

⅔ cup unsweetened cocoa powder

1½ teaspoons baking soda

½ teaspoon salt

4 tablespoons unsalted butter, at room temperature

4 tablespoons vegetable shortening

1 cup (packed) dark brown sugar

1 large egg

1 teaspoon vanilla extract

1 cup milk

red velvet whoopie

2½ cups all-purpose flour

1 cup cocoa powder

1 teaspoon baking powder

½ teaspoon baking soda

½ teaspoon salt

½ cup (1 stick) unsalted butter, at room temperature

½ cup vegetable shortening

½ cup (packed) brown sugar

1 cup granulated sugar

2 large eggs

2 teaspoons vanilla extract

½ ounce (one small bottle) red food coloring

1 cup buttermilk

Position a rack in the center of the oven and preheat the oven to 350°F. Line two baking sheets with parchment paper.

Sift together the flour, cocoa powder, baking powder, baking soda, and salt onto a sheet of waxed paper.

In the work bowl of a stand mixer fitted with the paddle attachment, beat together the butter, shortening, and both sugars on low speed until just combined. Increase the speed to medium and beat until fluffy and smooth, about 5 minutes. Add the eggs one at a time, beating well after each addition. Add the vanilla and red food coloring and beat just until blended.

Add half of the flour mixture and half of the buttermilk to the batter and beat on low until just incorporated. Scrape down the sides of the bowl. Add the remaining flour mixture and ½ cup buttermilk and beat until completely combined.

Using a spoon, drop about 1 tablespoon of batter onto one of the prepared baking sheets and repeat, spacing them at least 2 inches apart. Bake one sheet at a time for about 10 minutes each, or until the cakes spring back when pressed gently. Remove the baking sheet from the oven and let the cakes cool on the sheet for about 5 minutes before transferring them to a rack to cool completely.

Makes about 48 four-inch cakes.

Note: Sarah likes a lot of cocoa in her red velvet cake, so much so that her end product often looks more Black Velvet than Red Velvet. You can adjust the cocoa in this recipe, using as little as 1/4 cup, if you like less cocoa flavor and want a more intensely red whoopie pie.

Vanilla Wh oopie

2¼ cups all-purpose flour

1½ teaspoons baking powder

½ teaspoon salt

4 tablespoons unsalted butter, at room temperature

4 tablespoons vegetable shortening

½ cup granulated sugar

½ cup (packed) brown sugar

2 large eggs

½ cup buttermilk

2 tablespoons milk

1 teaspoon baking soda

1 teaspoon white vinegar

1 teaspoon vanilla extract (see Note)

Position a rack in the center of the oven and preheat the oven to 375°F. Line two baking sheets with parchment paper.

Sift together the flour, baking powder, and salt onto a sheet of waxed paper.

In the work bowl of a stand mixer fitted with the paddle attachment, beat together the butter, shortening, and both sugars until light and creamy, about 3 minutes. Add the eggs and the buttermilk and beat until combined.

In a measuring cup, combine the milk, baking soda, and vinegar. Add the milk mixture to the batter along with the flour mixture and beat on low until just combined. Add the vanilla and beat on medium for about 2 minutes until completely combined.

Using a spoon, drop about 1 tablespoon of batter onto one of the prepared baking sheets and repeat, spacing them at least 2 inches apart. Bake one sheet at a time for about 10 minutes each, or until the cakes begin to brown. Remove from the oven and let the cakes cool on the sheet for at least 5 minutes before transferring them to a rack to cool completely.

Makes about 48 two-inch cakes.

Note: For a more intense, luxurious flavor in your vanilla whoopie, use the seeds scraped from a vanilla bean in place of vanilla extract.

mocha whoopie

3 tablespoons instant espresso powder (or instant coffee)

2 tablespoons water

2¼ cups all-purpose flour

½ cup unsweetened cocoa powder

1½ teaspoons baking soda

½ teaspoon salt

4 tablespoons unsalted butter, at room temperature

4 tablespoons vegetable shortening

1 cup (packed) dark brown sugar

1 large egg

1 teaspoon vanilla extract

1 cup milk

Position a rack in the center of the oven and preheat the oven to 375°F. Line two baking sheets with parchment paper.

In a small bowl or cup, mix together the instant espresso powder and water and set aside.

Sift together the flour, cocoa powder, baking soda, and salt onto a sheet of waxed paper.

In the work bowl of a stand mixer fitted with the paddle attachment, beat together the butter, shortening, and brown sugar on low speed until just combined. Increase the speed to medium and beat until fluffy and smooth, about 3 minutes. Add the egg and vanilla and beat for another 2 minutes.

Add half of the flour mixture and half of the milk and beat on low until just incorporated. Scrape down the sides of the bowl. Add the espresso-water mixture and the remaining flour mixture and milk and beat until completely combined.

Using a spoon, drop about 1 tablespoon of batter onto one of the prepared baking sheets and repeat, spacing them at least 2 inches apart. Bake one sheet at a time for about 10 minutes each, or until the cakes spring back when touched. Remove the baking sheet from the oven and let the cakes cool on the sheet for about 5 minutes before transferring them to a rack to cool completely.

Makes about 48 two-inch cakes.

marbled whoopie

Position a rack in the center of the oven and preheat the oven to 375°F. Line two baking sheets with parchment paper.

Pour half of the vanilla batter into a large, shallow bowl. Add half of the chocolate batter. Draw a rubber spatula or large wooden spoon gently through the two batters, swirling them together to create marbling. (Do not mix them.) Repeat with remaining batter.

Using an ice cream scoop or a 2-tablespoon measuring spoon, drop the swirled batter one scoop at a time onto the prepared baking sheets, spacing them at least 2 inches apart. Bake one sheet at a time for about 15 minutes each, or until the cakes spring back when pressed gently. Remove from the oven and let the cakes cool on the sheet for at least 5 minutes before transferring them to a rack to cool completely.

Makes about 30 four-inch cakes.

1 recipe Classic Chocolate Whoopie batter (page 43)

1 recipe Vanilla Whoopie batter (page 46)

chocolate chip whoopie

2¼ cups all-purpose flour

1½ teaspoons baking powder

½ teaspoon salt

4 tablespoons unsalted butter, at room temperature

4 tablespoons vegetable shortening

½ cup granulated sugar

½ cup (packed) brown sugar

2 large eggs

½ cup buttermilk

2 tablespoons milk

1 teaspoon baking soda

1 teaspoon white vinegar

½ teaspoon vanilla extract

1 cup mini chocolate chips

Position a rack in the center of the oven and preheat the oven to 375°F. Line two baking sheets with parchment paper.

Sift together the flour, baking powder, and salt onto a sheet of waxed paper.

In the work bowl of a stand mixer fitted with the paddle attachment, beat together the butter, shortening, and both sugars and beat until light and creamy, about 3 minutes. Add the eggs and the buttermilk and beat until combined.

In a measuring cup, combine the milk, baking soda, and vinegar. Add the milk mixture to the batter along with the flour mixture and beat on low until just combined. Add the vanilla and beat on medium for about 2 minutes, until completely combined.

Using a wooden spoon, stir in the chocolate chips until just incorporated.

Using a spoon, drop about 1 tablespoon of batter onto one of the prepared baking sheets and repeat, spacing them at least 2 inches apart. Bake one sheet at a time for about 10 minutes each, or until the cakes begin to brown. Remove from the oven and let the cakes cool on the sheet for at least 5 minutes before transferring them to a rack to cool completely.

Makes about 48 two-inch cakes.

lemon whoopie

2¼ cups all-purpose flour

1½ teaspoons baking powder

1 teaspoon baking soda

½ teaspoon salt

4 tablespoons unsalted butter, at room temperature

4 tablespoons vegetable shortening

½ cup granulated sugar

½ cup (packed) brown sugar

2 large eggs

½ cup buttermilk

Grated zest of 1 lemon

2 tablespoons fresh lemon juice

½ teaspoon vanilla extract

Position a rack in the center of the oven and preheat the oven to 375°F. Line two baking sheets with parchment paper.

Sift together the flour, baking powder, baking soda, and salt onto a sheet of waxed paper.

In the work bowl of a stand mixer fitted with the paddle attachment, beat together the butter, shortening, and both sugars until light and creamy, about 3 minutes. Add the eggs and the buttermilk and beat until combined.

Add the lemon zest, lemon juice, and vanilla and beat on medium for about 2 minutes, until completely combined.

Using a spoon, drop about 1 tablespoon of batter onto one of the prepared baking sheets and repeat, spacing them at least 2 inches apart. Bake one sheet at a time for about 12 minutes each or until the cakes begin to brown. Remove from the oven and let the cakes cool on the sheet for at least 5 minutes before transferring them to a rack to cool completely.

Makes about 48 two-inch cakes.

gingerbread whoopie

Position a rack in the center of the oven and preheat the oven to 325°F. Line two baking sheets with parchment paper.

Sift together the flour, ginger, cinnamon, salt, baking soda, cloves, and nutmeg onto a sheet of waxed paper.

In the work bowl of a stand mixer fitted with the paddle attachment, beat together the butter, shortening, and brown sugar on low speed until just combined. Increase the speed to medium and beat until fluffy and smooth, about 5 minutes. Add the egg, beating well, then the molasses.

Add half of the flour mixture and half of the buttermilk to the batter and beat on low until just incorporated. Scrape down the sides of the bowl. Add the remaining flour mixture and buttermilk and beat until completely combined.

Using a spoon or 2-tablespoon scoop, drop about 2 table-spoons of batter onto one of the prepared baking sheets and repeat, spacing them at least 2 inches apart. Bake one sheet at a time for about 10 to 12 minutes each, or until the pies spring back when pressed gently. Remove from the oven and let the cakes cool on the sheet for about 5 minutes before transferring them to a rack to cool completely.

Makes about 30 four-inch cakes.

4 cups all-purpose flour

1½ teaspoons ground ginger

1½ teaspoons ground cinnamon

1 teaspoon salt

1 teaspoon baking soda

½ teaspoon ground cloves

¼ teaspoon ground nutmeg

½ cup (1 stick) unsalted butter, at room temperature

4 tablespoons vegetable shortening

¾ cup (packed) brown sugar

1 large egg

¾ cup molasses

¾ cup buttermilk

53

peanut butter whoopie

1¾ cups all-purpose flour

1 teaspoon baking soda

1 teaspoon baking powder

½ teaspoon salt

4 tablespoons (½ stick) unsalted butter, at room temperature

4 tablespoons (½ stick) vegetable shortening

½ cup (packed) brown sugar

½ cup creamy or crunchy peanut butter

1 teaspoon vanilla extract

2 large eggs

1½ cups buttermilk

Position a rack in the center of the oven and preheat the oven to 375°F. Line two baking sheets with parchment paper.

Sift together the flour, baking soda, baking powder, and salt onto a sheet of waxed paper.

In the work bowl of a stand mixer fitted with the paddle attachment, beat together the butter, shortening, brown sugar, peanut butter, and vanilla until light and creamy, about 3 minutes. Add the eggs, one at a time, stopping the mixer to scrape down the sides of the bowl between additions.

Add ½ of the flour mixture, beating on medium speed, just until combined. Stop the mixer and add ½ of the buttermilk. Beat on medium speed until combined. Repeat with the remaining flour mixture and buttermilk, beating until thoroughly combined and scraping down the sides of the bowl.

Using a spoon or 2-tablespoon scoop, drop about 2 tablespoons of batter onto one of the prepared baking sheets and repeat, spacing them at least 2 inches apart. Bake one sheet at a time for about 18 minutes each, or until the cakes begin to brown at the edges and are firm to the touch. Remove from the oven and let the cakes cool on the sheet for at least 5 minutes before transferring them to a rack to cool completely.

Makes about 24 four-inch cakes.

54

banana whoopie

Position a rack in the center of the oven and preheat the oven to 350°F. Line two baking sheets with parchment paper.

Sift together both flours, baking soda, and salt onto a sheet of waxed paper.

In the work bowl of a stand mixer fitted with the paddle attachment, beat together the butter, shortening, sugar, and vanilla until light and creamy, about 3 minutes. Add the eggs and beat until combined.

Add the bananas and the pecans (if using) and beat on medium for about 2 minutes, until completely combined.

Using a spoon, drop about 1 tablespoon of batter onto one of the prepared baking sheets and repeat, spacing them at least 2 inches apart. Bake one sheet at a time for about 10 minutes each, or until the cakes begin to brown. Remove from the oven and let the cakes cool on the sheet for at least 5 minutes before transferring them to a rack to cool completely.

Makes about 48 two-inch cakes.

Note: This is a great recipe to add a tablespoon or two of flax meal or wheat germ to amp up the whole grain factor. Go ahead and eat two—it's healthy!

1 cup all-purpose flour

1 cup whole wheat flour

1 teaspoon baking soda

½ teaspoon salt

4 tablespoons unsalted butter, at room temperature

4 tablespoons vegetable shortening

¾ cup granulated sugar

1 teaspoon vanilla extract

2 large eggs

3 very ripe bananas, mashed

¾ cup chopped toasted pecans (optional)

pistachio-cardamom whoopie

Position a rack in the center of the oven and preheat the oven to 350°F. Line two baking sheets with parchment paper.

Sift together the flour, baking powder, cardamom, and salt onto a sheet of waxed paper.

In the work bowl of a stand mixer fitted with the paddle attachment, beat together the butter and both sugars on low speed until just combined. Increase the speed to medium and beat until fluffy and smooth, about 5 minutes. Add the egg, beating well. Add the vanilla.

Add half of the flour mixture and half of the buttermilk to the batter and beat on low until just incorporated. Scrape down the sides of the bowl. Add the remaining flour mixture and ½ cup buttermilk and beat until completely combined. Add the pistachios and mix just until combined.

Using a small ice-cream scoop or 2-tablespoon scoop, drop about 2 tablespoons of batter onto one of the prepared baking sheets and repeat, spacing them at least 2 inches apart. Bake one sheet at a time for about 10 minutes each, or until the cakes begin to brown. Let the cakes cool on the sheet for at least 5 minutes before transferring them to a rack to cool completely.

Makes about 30 four-inch cakes.

Note: This recipe is a template for your nut-and-spice whoopie. You can substitute ground hazelnuts, almonds, or macadamia nuts for the pistachios and cinnamon, ginger, or other ground spices for the cardamom.

3 cups all-purpose flour

1½ teaspoons baking powder

1 teaspoon ground cardamom

½ teaspoon salt

½ cup (1 stick) butter, softened

¾ cup granulated sugar

¾ cup (packed) brown sugar

1 large egg

1 teaspoon vanilla extract

1 cup buttermilk

¾ cup ground pistachios

graham cracker whoopie

1½ cups graham flour

¾ cup all-purpose flour

1½ teaspoons baking powder

½ teaspoon salt

4 tablespoons unsalted butter, at room temperature

4 tablespoons vegetable shortening

1 cup (packed) dark brown sugar

2 large eggs

½ cup buttermilk

2 tablespoons milk

1 teaspoon baking soda

1 teaspoon white vinegar

1 teaspoon vanilla extract

Position a rack in the center of the oven and preheat the oven to 375°F. Line two baking sheets with parchment paper.

In a medium bowl, stir together both flours, baking powder, and salt.

In the work bowl of a stand mixer fitted with the paddle attachment, beat together the butter, shortening, and brown sugar until light and creamy, about 3 minutes. Add the eggs and the buttermilk and beat until combined.

In a measuring cup, combine the milk, baking soda, and vinegar. Add the milk mixture to the batter along with the flour mixture and beat on low speed until just combined. Add the vanilla and beat on medium speed for about 2 minutes, until completely combined.

Using a spoon, drop about 1 tablespoon of batter onto one of the prepared baking sheets and repeat, spacing them at least 2 inches apart. Bake one sheet at a time for about 10 minutes each, or until the cakes begin to brown. Remove from the oven and let the cakes cool on the sheet for at least 5 minutes before transferring them to a rack to cool completely.

Makes about 48 two-inch cakes.

Note: This is the basis of the S'mores Whoopie, which may be Amy's favorite. Spread with Marshmallow Cream and Chocolate Ganache, but if you're in a hurry a dollop of Marshmallow Fluff and a square of chocolate is a fine substitute.

oatmeal wh  opie

Preheat the oven to 350°F. Line two baking sheets with parchment paper.

In the work bowl of a stand mixer fitted with the paddle attachment, beat together the butter and both sugars on low speed. Increase the speed to medium and beat until fluffy and smooth, about 3 minutes. Beat in the eggs one at a time. Add the vanilla and beat until light and creamy, about 3 minutes.

In a food processor or blender, process ¾ cup of the oatmeal until it resembles whole grain flour. Transfer the ground oatmeal to a medium bowl and add the remaining oatmeal, flour, baking soda, cinnamon, and salt. Add the oatmeal mixture to the butter-sugar mixture and beat on low speed until just combined.

Using a spoon, drop about 1 tablespoon of batter onto one of the prepared baking sheets and repeat, spacing them at least 2 inches apart. Bake one sheet at a time for about 11 minutes each or until the cookies begin to brown. Remove from the oven and let the cakes cool on the sheet for about 5 minutes before transferring them to a cooling rack to cool completely.

Makes about 48 two-inch cakes.

4 tablespoons unsalted butter, at room temperature

½ cup (packed) brown sugar

¼ cup granulated sugar

2 large eggs

1 teaspoon vanilla extract

1½ cups rolled oats (not fast-cooking)

¾ cup all-purpose flour

½ teaspoon baking soda

½ teaspoon ground cinnamon

1 teaspoon salt

½ cup raisins (optional)

½ cup chopped pecans or nuts of your choice (optional)

pumpkin whoopie

2¼ cups all-purpose flour

1 teaspoon baking powder

½ teaspoon baking soda

1 tablespoon ground cinnamon

1½ teaspoons ground ginger

1 teaspoon ground allspice

1 teaspoon ground nutmeg

½ teaspoon salt

1 cup brown sugar

½ cup unsalted butter, at room temperature

1½ cups solid pack pumpkin

1 egg

1 teaspoon vanilla

Position a rack in the center of the oven and preheat the oven to 350°F. Line two baking sheets with parchment paper.

Sift together the flour, baking powder, baking soda, cinnamon, ginger, allspice, nutmeg, and salt onto a sheet of waxed paper.

In the work bowl of a stand mixer fitted with the paddle attachment, beat together the brown sugar and butter on low speed until just combined. Add the pumpkin, then the egg, beating well. Add the vanilla and beat until combined.

Add the flour mixture and beat on low until just incorporated, scraping down the sides of the bowl.

Using a small ice-cream scoop or 2-tablespoon scoop, drop about 2 tablespoons of batter onto one of the prepared baking sheets and repeat, spacing them at least 2 inches apart. Bake one sheet at a time for about 15 minutes each, or until the cakes begin to crack and are firm to the touch. Let the cakes cool on the sheet for at least 5 minutes before transferring them to a rack to cool completely.

Makes about 30 four-inch cakes.

carrot cake whoopie

2 cups all-purpose flour

1½ teaspoons baking soda

1 teaspoon baking powder

1 teaspoon ground cinnamon

1 teaspoon ground ginger

½ teaspoon ground nutmeg

½ teaspoon salt

½ cup (1 stick) unsalted butter, at room temperature (see Note)

½ cup (packed) light brown sugar

½ cup granulated sugar

2 large eggs

1 teaspoon vanilla extract

2 medium carrots, grated (about 2 cups)

1 cup raisins or pecans

½ cup shredded coconut (optional)

Position rack in the center of the oven and preheat the oven to 350°F. Line two baking sheets with parchment paper.

Sift together the flour, baking soda, baking powder, cinnamon, ginger, nutmeg, and salt onto a sheet of waxed paper.

In the work bowl of a stand mixer fitted with the paddle attachment, beat together the butter and both sugars until light and creamy, about 5 minutes. Scrape down the sides of the bowl with a rubber spatula, then add the eggs and the vanilla and beat until combined. Mix in the flour mixture just until combined, then add the carrots, raisins, and coconut (if using). Chill the batter in the refrigerator for at least 1 hour.

Using a small ice-cream scoop or 2-tablespoon scoop, drop about 2 tablespoons of batter onto one of the prepared baking sheets and repeat, spacing them at least 2 inches apart. Bake one sheet at a time for about 20 minutes each or until the cakes spring back when pressed gently. Remove from the oven and let the cakes cool on the sheet for at least 5 minutes before transferring them to a rack to cool completely.

Makes about 30 four-inch cakes.

Note: Sometimes butter is 100 percent necessary, such as in this recipe, where it adds richness and contributes to the soft, cakey texture. Because of the moistness of the ingredients, this batter must be chilled, and these cakes take a little bit longer to bake.

vegan chocolate whoopie

Position a rack in the center of the oven and preheat the oven to 375°F. Line two baking sheets with parchment paper.

In a small bowl, whisk together the rice milk and vinegar (the mixture will quickly look curdled; that's okay) and set aside. In another small bowl, whisk together the egg replacement powder and the hot water and set aside.

Sift together the flour, cocoa powder, baking soda, baking powder, and salt onto a sheet of waxed paper. In the work bowl of a stand mixer fitted with the paddle attachment, beat together the butter substitute and the brown sugar on low speed until creamy, about 3 minutes. Increase the speed to medium and beat until fluffy and smooth, about 3 minutes. Add the egg replacement mixture and the vanilla and beat on medium speed for 1 minute.

Add half of the flour mixture and half of the rice milk mixture to the batter and beat on low speed until just incorporated. Scrape down the sides of the bowl. Add the remaining flour mixture and rice milk mixture and beat until thoroughly combined.

Using a spoon, drop about 1 tablespoon of batter onto one of the prepared baking sheets and repeat, spacing them at least 2 inches apart. Bake one sheet at a time for about 12 minutes each or until the cakes spring back when pressed gently. Remove from the oven and let the cakes cool on the sheet for about 5 minutes before transferring them to a rack to cool completely.

1 cup rice milk

1 tablespoon white vinegar

2 tablespoons egg alternative, preferably Ener-G Egg Replacement Powder

4 tablespoons hot water

1⅓ cups all-purpose flour

⅔ cup cocoa powder

1 teaspoon baking soda

½ teaspoon baking powder

¼ teaspoon salt

⅓ cup dairy-free butter substitute, preferably Smart Balance Buttery Spread

1 cup (packed) brown sugar

1 teaspoon vanilla extract

Makes about 48 two-inch cakes.

65

Vegan Vanilla Whoopie

1 cup rice milk

1 tablespoon white vinegar

2 tablespoons egg alternative, preferably Ener-G Egg Replacement Powder

4 tablespoons hot water

2 cups all-purpose flour

1 teaspoon baking soda

½ teaspoon baking powder

½ teaspoon salt

⅓ cup dairy-free butter substitute, preferably Smart Balance Buttery Spread

1 cup (packed) dark brown sugar

1 teaspoon vanilla extract

Position a rack in the center of the oven and preheat the oven to 375°F. Line two baking sheets with parchment paper.

In a small bowl, whisk together the rice milk and vinegar (the mixture will quickly look curdled; that's okay) and set aside. In another small bowl, whisk together the egg replacement powder and the hot water and set aside.

Sift together the flour, baking soda, baking powder, and salt onto a sheet of waxed paper. In the work bowl of a stand mixer fitted with the paddle attachment, beat together the butter substitute and the brown sugar on low speed until creamy, about 3 minutes. Increase the speed to medium and beat until fluffy and smooth, about 3 minutes. Add the egg replacement mixture and the vanilla and beat on medium speed for 1 minute.

Add half of the flour mixture and half of the rice milk mixture to the batter and beat on low speed until just incorporated. Scrape down the sides of the bowl. Add the remaining flour mixture and rice milk mixture and beat until thoroughly combined.

Using a spoon, drop about 1 tablespoon of batter onto one of the prepared baking sheets and repeat, spacing them at least 2 inches apart. Bake one sheet at a time for about 10 minutes each or until the cakes spring back when pressed gently. Remove from the oven and let the cakes cool on the sheet for about 5 minutes before transferring them to a rack to cool completely.

Makes about 48 two-inch cakes.

Gluten-free and vegan

We think whoopie pies are so great that everyone should be able to try them. So we came up with two recipes for gluten-free versions that are pretty close to the original. We opted to use a mix from Bob's Red Mill, but you could also combine a few non-wheat flours—choose from among sorghum flour, rice flour, garbanzo bean flour, potato starch, tapioca flour, and fava bean flour—and create your own custom blend.

We used vanilla in our gluten-free recipes. Since vanilla contains alcohol and alcohol is made from grain, those who are super-sensitive to gluten might want to leave it out.

Switch out the eggs with Ener-G Egg Replacement Powder and the milk with rice or almond milk and you've got a VEGAN, gluten-free whoopie!

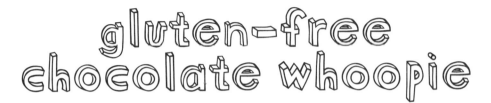

gluten-free chocolate whoopie

2¼ cups gluten-free all-purpose flour (such as Bob's Red Mill Gluten Free All Purpose Baking Flour; see page 112)

¾ cup unsweetened cocoa powder

1½ teaspoons baking powder

1 teaspoon salt

½ teaspoon baking soda

½ teaspoon xantham gum (such as Bob's Red Mill; see page 112)

4 tablespoons unsalted butter, at room temperature

4 tablespoons vegetable shortening

½ cup granulated sugar

½ cup (packed) dark brown sugar

2 large eggs

1 teaspoon vanilla extract

1 cup milk

Position a rack in the center of the oven and preheat the oven to 375°F. Line two baking sheets with parchment paper.

In a medium bowl, stir together the flour, cocoa powder, baking powder, salt, baking soda, and xantham gum.

In the work bowl of a stand mixer fitted with the paddle attachment, beat together the butter, shortening, and both sugars until light and creamy, about 3 minutes. Add the eggs and vanilla and beat until combined.

Add half of the flour mixture and half of the milk to the batter and beat on low speed until just incorporated. Scrape down the sides of the bowl. Add the remaining flour mixture and ½ cup milk and beat until thoroughly combined.

Using a spoon, drop about 1 tablespoon of batter onto one of the prepared baking sheets and repeat, spacing them at least 2 inches apart. Bake one sheet at a time for about 12 minutes each or until the cakes begin to brown. Remove from the oven and let the cakes cool on the sheet for at least 5 minutes before transferring them to a rack to cool completely.

Makes about 48 two-inch cakes.

Note: Xantham gum is the secret weapon that mimics the properties of gluten and keeps these whoopies from spreading into a big mess while they bake.

gluten-free vanilla whoopie

Position a rack in the center of the oven and preheat the oven to 375°F. Line two baking sheets with parchment paper.

In a medium bowl, stir together the flour, baking powder, salt, and xantham gum.

In the work bowl of a stand mixer fitted with the paddle attachment, beat together the butter, shortening, and both sugars until light and creamy, about 3 minutes. Add the eggs and the buttermilk and beat until combined.

In a small measuring cup, combine the milk, baking soda, and vinegar and add to the batter along with the flour mixture; beat on low until just combined. Add the vanilla and beat on medium until completely combined, about 2 minutes.

Using a spoon, drop about 1 tablespoon of batter onto one of the prepared baking sheets and repeat, spacing them at least 2 inches apart. Bake one sheet at a time for about 10 minutes or until the cakes begin to brown. Remove from the oven and let the cakes cool on the sheet for at least 5 minutes before transferring them to a rack to cool completely.

Makes about 48 two-inch cakes.

2¼ cups gluten-free all-purpose flour (such as Bob's Red Mill Gluten Free All Purpose Baking Flour; see page 112)

1½ teaspoons baking powder

½ teaspoon salt

½ teaspoon xantham gum (such as Bob's Red Mill; see page 112)

4 tablespoons unsalted butter, at room temperature

4 tablespoons vegetable shortening

½ cup granulated sugar

½ cup (packed) dark brown sugar

2 large eggs

½ cup buttermilk

2 tablespoons milk

1 teaspoon baking soda

1 teaspoon white vinegar

1 teaspoon vanilla extract

wh opie cake

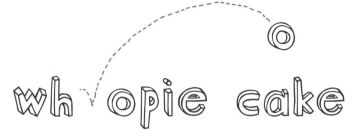

Position a rack in the center of the oven and preheat the oven to 350°F. Line two baking sheets with parchment paper.

Sift together the flour, cocoa powder, baking soda, and salt onto a sheet of waxed paper.

In the work bowl of a stand mixer fitted with the paddle attachment, beat together the butter, shortening, and brown sugar on low speed until just combined. Increase the speed to medium and beat until fluffy and smooth, about 3 minutes. Add the eggs and vanilla and beat for another 2 minutes.

Add half of the flour mixture and half of the milk to the batter and beat on low speed until just incorporated. Scrape down the sides of the bowl. Add the remaining flour mixture and ½ cup milk and beat until thoroughly combined.

Divide the batter between the two prepared baking sheets, spreading evenly to form a circle about 9 inches wide. Bake one sheet at a time for about 15 minutes each or until the cakes spring back when pressed gently and a toothpick inserted into the center comes out clean. Remove from the oven and let the cakes cool on the sheet for about 5 minutes before transferring to a rack to cool completely.

1⅔ cups all-purpose flour

⅔ cup unsweetened cocoa powder

1½ teaspoons baking soda

½ teaspoon salt

4 tablespoons unsalted butter, at room temperature

4 tablespoons vegetable shortening

1 cup (packed) dark brown sugar

2 large eggs

1 teaspoon vanilla extract

1 cup milk

Makes 2 nine-inch cakes (for 1 assembled cake-size whoopie pie).

71

jalapeño cornbread whoopie

Position a rack in the center of the oven and preheat the oven to 375°F. Line two baking sheets with parchment paper.

In a medium bowl, stir together the flour, cornmeal, brown sugar, baking powder, and salt. In the work bowl of a stand mixer fitted with the paddle attachment, beat together the buttermilk, butter, and egg on low speed until just combined. Increase the speed to medium and beat until thoroughly combined, about 3 minutes. Add the flour mixture and the chopped chiles to the batter and beat on low until just combined.

Using a spoon, drop about 1 tablespoon of batter onto one of the prepared baking sheets and repeat, spacing them at least 2 inches apart. Bake one sheet at a time for about 12 minutes each or until the cakes begin to brown around the edges. Remove from the oven and let the cakes cool on the sheet for about 5 minutes before transferring them to a rack to cool completely.

Makes about 48 two-inch cakes.

Note: Try adding ½ cup of shredded cheddar and leaving out the jalapeño. For the filling, spread with chutney and top with a slice of ham for a whoopie lunch.

1¼ cups all-purpose flour

1 cup cornmeal

¼ cup (packed) brown sugar

2 teaspoons baking powder

1 teaspoon salt

1 cup buttermilk

4 tablespoons unsalted butter, at room temperature

1 large egg

2 jalapeño peppers, seeded and finely chopped

the
creamy
fillings

classic marshmallow

1 7oz
jar →

1½ cups Marshmallow Fluff (or other prepared marshmallow cream, which will do in a pinch)

1¼ cups vegetable shortening

1 cup confectioners' sugar

1 tablespoon vanilla extract

In the work bowl of a stand mixer fitted with the paddle attachment, beat together the Marshmallow Fluff and the vegetable shortening, starting on low and increasing to medium speed until the mixture is smooth and fluffy, about 3 minutes. Reduce mixer speed to low, add the confectioners' sugar and the vanilla, and beat until incorporated. Increase mixer speed to medium and beat until fluffy, about 3 minutes more.

76

chocolate buttercream

In the work bowl of a stand mixer fitted with the paddle attachment, beat together the confectioners' sugar, cocoa, and butter, starting on low and increasing to medium speed, until the mixture is crumbly, about 1 minute. Add the heavy cream, vanilla, and salt and beat on high until smooth, about 3 minutes.

1⅓ cups confectioners' sugar

½ cup cocoa powder

4 tablespoons unsalted butter, at room temperature

3 tablespoons heavy (whipping) cream

1 teaspoon vanilla extract

½ teaspoon salt

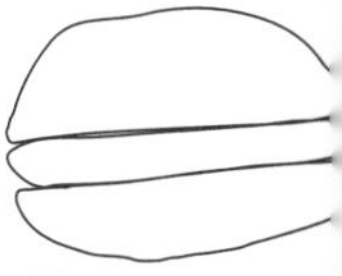

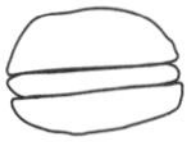

79

classic cream cheese

4 ounces cream cheese, at room temperature

4 tablespoons unsalted butter, at room temperature

3½ cups (one 16-ounce box) confectioners' sugar

1 teaspoon vanilla extract

In the work bowl of a stand mixer fitted with the paddle attachment, beat together the cream cheese and butter on medium speed. Add the sugar and beat on low speed until combined. Add the vanilla and increase the speed to medium; beat until creamy and smooth, about 4 minutes.

classic buttercream

In the work bowl of a stand mixer fitted with the paddle attachment, beat together the confectioners' sugar with the butter, starting on low and increasing to medium speed, until the mixture is crumbly, about 1 minute. Add the heavy cream, vanilla, and salt and beat on high speed until smooth, about 3 minutes.

3 cups confectioners' sugar

½ cup (1 stick) unsalted butter, at room temperature

3 to 4 tablespoons heavy (whipping) cream

1 teaspoon vanilla extract

Pinch of salt

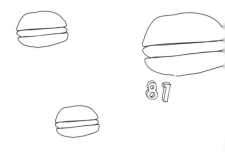

81

chocolate ganache

8 ounces semisweet or bittersweet chocolate chips or 8 ounces dark chocolate, finely chopped

½ cup heavy (whipping) cream

Put the chocolate in a large, heatproof bowl. Heat the cream in a large, heavy saucepan over medium heat just until it bubbles. Pour the hot cream over the chocolate in the bowl and let it sit for about 10 minutes, until the chocolate is melted. Stir with a wooden spoon or spatula until smooth. Allow the mixture to rest at room temperature until firm enough to spread, about 2 hours. You may also refrigerate the mixture for about 30 minutes, until it is firm enough to spread, stirring every 10 minutes.

Note: Ground spices, such as cayenne pepper, ginger, or cinnamon, can be added to ganache. A rule of thumb: add up to ½ teaspoon of most ground spices, or to taste. But use a lighter hand with the hot stuff. Just add a pinch, or up to ⅛ teaspoon cayenne or habañero powder.

82

whipped chocolate ganache

Put the chocolate in a large, heatproof bowl. In a large, heavy-bottomed saucepan over medium heat, heat the cream until it bubbles. Pour the hot cream over the chopped chocolate and let it sit for about 10 minutes, until the chocolate is melted. Add the salt and vanilla and stir with a wooden spoon or silicone spatula just to combine.

Refrigerate the ganache for at least 1 hour and up to 24 hours, until it is firm. Using a hand mixer or stand mixer, beat the ganache at medium speed until it is softened and lighter in color, about 2 minutes.

Note: Good-quality chocolate makes a major difference in the taste of your ganache. When you're baking for loved ones, don't cheap out.

1 pound bittersweet chocolate, chopped

2½ cups heavy (whipping) cream

Pinch of salt, preferably sea salt

1 tablespoon vanilla extract, rum, or rosewater

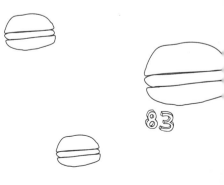

mint buttercream

2 cups confectioners' sugar

4 tablespoons unsalted butter, at room temperature

3 tablespoons heavy (whipping) cream

2 teaspoons vanilla extract

½ teaspoon mint extract

½ teaspoon salt

In the work bowl of a stand mixer fitted with the paddle attachment, beat together the confectioners' sugar and the butter, starting on low and increasing to medium speed, until the mixture is crumbly, about 1 minute. Add the heavy cream, vanilla, mint extract, and salt and beat on high until smooth, about 3 minutes.

honey buttercream

In the work bowl of a stand mixer fitted with the paddle attachment, beat together the confectioners' sugar and the butter, starting on low and increasing to medium speed, until the mixture is crumbly, about 1 minute. Add the heavy cream, honey, lemon juice, and salt and beat on high speed until smooth, about 3 minutes.

3 cups confectioners' sugar

½ cup (1 stick) unsalted butter, at room temperature

3 to 4 tablespoons heavy (whipping) cream

2 teaspoons honey

1 teaspoon fresh lemon juice

Pinch of salt

85

rosewater buttercream

2 cups confectioners' sugar

4 tablespoons unsalted butter, at room temperature

3 tablespoons heavy (whipping) cream

1 teaspoon rosewater or rose essence

1 teaspoon vanilla extract

⅛ teaspoon salt

3 to 4 drops red food coloring

In the work bowl of a stand mixer fitted with the paddle attachment, beat together the confectioners' sugar and the butter, starting on low and increasing to medium speed, until the mixture is crumbly, about 1 minute. Add the heavy cream, rosewater, vanilla, salt, and red food coloring and beat on high until smooth, about 3 minutes.

salty peanut butter

In the work bowl of a stand mixer fitted with the paddle attachment, beat together the peanut butter and butter on low speed until smooth and creamy. Add the confectioners' sugar and the salt and beat on low to incorporate. Increase the speed to medium and beat until the filling is light and fluffy, about 4 minutes.

Note: Yes, it's salty, but it doesn't have to be so salty. If you leave out the ½ teaspoon of salt, you end up with a not-too-sweet, respectably nutty filling.

¾ cup creamy or crunchy peanut butter

¾ cup (6 tablespoons) unsalted butter, at room temperature

¾ cup confectioners' sugar

½ teaspoon salt

87

coconut cream

4 tablespoons unsalted butter, at room temperature

1¾ cups confectioners' sugar

3 tablespoons sweetened shredded coconut

2 tablespoons unsweetened shredded coconut

3 tablespoons coconut milk

½ teaspoon vanilla extract

In the work bowl of a stand mixer fitted with the paddle attachment, beat together the butter and sugar on low speed until combined. Add the sweetened coconut, unsweetened coconut, coconut milk, and vanilla and beat on low until smooth, about 5 minutes.

Variation: Add 1 tablespoon solid coconut oil (see Ingredients & Sources, page 111) for a more intense coconut flavor.

malted buttercream

In the work bowl of a stand mixer fitted with the paddle attachment, beat together the butter and sugar on low speed until combined. Add the Ovaltine powder, heavy cream, and vanilla and beat until smooth, about 3 minutes.

Note: You can use malted milk powder in place of the Ovaltine in this recipe.

4 tablespoons unsalted butter, at room temperature

1¾ cups confectioners' sugar

4 tablespoons Ovaltine powder

3 tablespoons heavy (whipping) cream

½ teaspoon vanilla extract

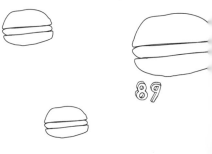

89

salted caramel

½ cup sugar

2 tablespoons water

2 tablespoons heavy (whipping) cream

Coarse sea salt

Combine the sugar and the water in a small saucepan over medium-high heat until the sugar dissolves, swirling the saucepan gently (do not stir). Allow the mixture to darken until the sugar turns a deep amber color, about 5 minutes. Remove from the heat and whisk in the cream. Be careful—the cream will sputter and bubble when added. Whisk the caramel until smooth and set aside to cool for 10 minutes. Add a large pinch of sea salt, stir to combine, and allow to rest another 30 minutes before using.

Note: We like to use coarse sea salt for its texture. These large grains won't dissolve homogenously throughout the caramel, and it's quite a tasty surprise to hit a salty pocket in a sea of sweet.

candied ginger

In the work bowl of a stand mixer fitted with the paddle attachment, beat the butter on low speed for 1 minute. Increase the speed to medium and beat until creamy, about 3 more minutes. Add the salt, candied ginger, and ground ginger and mix on low until incorporated. Add the confectioners' sugar, 1 cup at a time, and mix on low until it starts to form a ball. Add the cream, 1 tablespoon at a time, and beat on low for 1 minute. Increase speed to medium and beat for 4 minutes, occasionally stopping to scrape down the sides of the bowl, until the mixture is light and fluffy.

4 tablespoons (½ stick) unsalted butter, at room temperature

½ teaspoon salt

¼ cup chopped candied ginger

½ teaspoon ground ginger

3 cups confectioners' sugar

2 to 3 tablespoons heavy (whipping) cream

dulce de leche

Two 14-ounce cans
sweetened condensed milk

Position a rack in the center of the oven and preheat the oven to 400°F.

Pour the sweetened condensed milk into a pie plate or other shallow, wide oven-proof container and cover tightly with aluminum foil. Set the pie plate inside a larger baking pan and place in the oven. Add enough boiling water to the baking pan to reach halfway up the side of the pie plate, without getting any water in the pie plate.

Bake for at least 1 hour. Carefully pull up the foil to check and, using a spoon, stir to see if the milk has thickened and turned a rich caramel color. Cover with the foil and continue to bake, checking every 10 minutes or so until it's done. Add more boiling water as needed to keep the level at least halfway up the side of the pie plate.

Transfer the pie plate to a rack and let cool for about 2 hours. Use a hand mixer or a wooden spoon to beat the mixture until smooth. It should be thick enough to support a metal spoon without sinking.

maple

In the work bowl of a stand mixer, beat the butter on low speed until creamy. Add the sugar, ½ cup at a time, with the mixer on low until incorporated. Add the milk, maple syrup, and maple flavoring (if using), and beat on medium for 3 to 4 minutes to incorporate, scraping down the sides of the bowl periodically.

Note: Purists may want to leave out the maple flavoring, so we kept it optional. It does give the finished filling a much more intense maple flavor.

½ cup (1 stick) unsalted butter, at room temperature

2 cups confectioners' sugar

1 tablespoon milk

2 tablespoons pure maple syrup

⅛ teaspoon maple flavoring (optional)

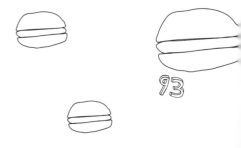

93

maple-bacon

4 thick strips bacon, cut into ¼-inch dice

½ cup (1 stick) unsalted butter, at room temperature

2 cups confectioners' sugar

3 tablespoons heavy (whipping) cream

1 tablespoon sour cream

1 tablespoon vanilla extract

1 tablespoon pure maple syrup

⅛ teaspoon maple flavoring

½ teaspoon salt

In a medium skillet, cook the bacon over medium heat until crisp. Using a slotted spoon, transfer the bacon to a paper-towel-lined plate to drain and cool.

In the work bowl of a stand mixer fitted with the paddle attachment, beat together the butter and sugar on low speed until combined. Add the heavy cream, sour cream, vanilla, maple syrup, maple flavoring, and salt and beat on low until smooth, about 3 minutes.

Using a wooden spoon, stir in the bacon until just combined.

root beer

In the work bowl of a stand mixer fitted with the paddle attachment, beat together the Marshmallow Fluff and the vegetable shortening, starting on low and increasing to medium speed until the mixture is smooth and fluffy, about 3 minutes. Add the confectioners' sugar and the root beer flavoring and beat on low until incorporated, then increase the speed to medium and beat until fluffy, about 3 more minutes.

Note: This recipe uses the Classic Marshmallow filling as a template, but you can also make an excellent root beer filling by adding 1 teaspoon root beer extract to the Classic Butter-cream filling (page 81). Even better, add 1 teaspoon root beer or 1 tablespoon root beer Schnapps to the Chocolate Ganache or Whipped Chocolate Ganache filling for a thick and fudgy root beer filling.

1½ cups Marshmallow Fluff (or other prepared marshmallow cream, which will do in a pinch)

1¼ cups vegetable shortening

1 cup confectioners' sugar

4 tablespoons root beer or root beer Schnapps, or 1 teaspoon root beer extract

orange cream cheese

1¼ cups confectioners' sugar

6 ounces cream cheese, at room temperature

Grated zest of 1 orange

½ cup (1 stick) butter, at room temperature

½ teaspoon vanilla extract

1 teaspoon fresh orange juice

Sift confectioners' sugar onto a sheet of parchment paper.

In the work bowl of a stand mixer fitted with the paddle attachment, beat together the cream cheese and sugar on low speed until combined. Add the orange zest, butter, vanilla, and orange juice. Increase the speed to medium and beat until creamy and smooth, about 4 minutes.

lemon mascarpone

Sift confectioners' sugar onto a sheet of parchment paper.

In the work bowl of a stand mixer fitted with the paddle attachment, beat together the mascarpone and butter. Add the sugar on low speed. Increase speed to medium and beat until fluffy, about 3 minutes. Add the lemon extract and zest (if using) and beat until combined.

3 cups confectioners' sugar

½ cup mascarpone cheese, at room temperature

4 tablespoons butter, at room temperature

1½ teaspoons lemon extract

1 teaspoon grated lemon zest (optional)

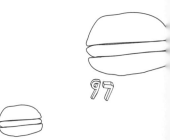

tiramisù cream

3 cups confectioners' sugar

½ cup mascarpone cheese, at room temperature

4 tablespoons butter, at room temperature

1 tablespoon espresso or strong-brewed coffee or ½ teaspoon instant espresso powder

½ teaspoon vanilla extract

1 teaspoon rum or Marsala (optional)

Sift the sugar onto a sheet of parchment paper.

In the work bowl of a stand mixer fitted with the paddle attachment, beat together the mascarpone and butter. Add the sifted sugar and beat on low speed. Increase speed to medium and beat until fluffy, about 3 minutes. Add the espresso, vanilla, and rum (if using), and beat until combined.

strawberry buttercream

In the work bowl of a food processor, pulse the sugar and the strawberries until the strawberries are crushed into very small pieces.

In the work bowl of a stand mixer fitted with the paddle attachment, beat together the sugar-strawberry mixture, butter, vanilla, Marshmallow Fluff, flour, and milk, starting on low speed and increasing to medium. Scrape down the sides of the bowl occasionally and continue to beat until the mixture is smooth and creamy, about 4 minutes.

Note: Freeze-dried strawberries are a great ingredient in frostings and other fillings like this because they add a punch of intense, pure flavor without adding moisture.

Freeze-dried strawberries and other freeze-dried fruits and vegetables can be found at gourmet grocery stores like Whole Foods. We used Just Strawberries (see Ingredients & Sources, page 111). Dried fruit can also be used but expect the fruit pieces to be bigger in the final filling and have a less intense fruit flavor.

2 cups confectioners' sugar

½ cup freeze-dried strawberries (see Note)

6 tablespoons (¾ stick) unsalted butter, at room temperature

1 tablespoon vanilla extract

3 tablespoons Marshmallow Fluff (or other prepared marshmallow cream, which will do in a pinch)

2 tablespoons all-purpose flour

2 tablespoons milk

peachy marshmallow cream

1½ cups confectioners' sugar

½ cup freeze-dried peaches (see Ingredients & Sources, page 111)

4 tablespoons unsalted butter, at room temperature

4 tablespoons Marshmallow Fluff (or other prepared marshmallow cream, which will do in a pinch)

2 tablespoons milk

1 tablespoon vanilla extract

In the work bowl of a food processor, pulse the sugar and the peaches until the peaches are crushed into very small pieces.

In the work bowl of a stand mixer fitted with the paddle attachment, beat together the sugar-peach mixture, butter, marshmallow fluff, milk, and vanilla, starting on low speed and increasing to medium. Scrape down the sides of the bowl occasionally and continue to beat until the mixture is smooth and creamy, about 4 minutes.

banana

In the work bowl of a stand mixer fitted with the paddle attachment, beat the butter, starting on low and increasing to medium speed, until creamy, about 2 minutes. Add the salt, banana, lime juice, and vanilla and beat on medium until smooth, about 1 minute. Add the confectioners' sugar, 1 cup at a time, and beat on low until incorporated. Increase the speed to medium and beat until light and fluffy, about 3 more minutes. Add more confectioners' sugar as needed to get the consistency you want.

4 tablespoons (½ stick) unsalted butter, at room temperature

½ teaspoon salt

½ cup very ripe mashed banana (about 1)

¼ teaspoon fresh lime juice

½ teaspoon vanilla extract

3½ to 4 cups confectioners' sugar

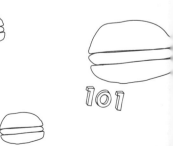

101

matcha buttercream

In the work bowl of a stand mixer fitted with the paddle attachment, beat together the sugar and the butter, starting on low and increasing to medium speed, until the mixture is crumbly, about 1 minute. Add the heavy cream, vanilla, salt, and matcha powder and beat on high until smooth, about 3 minutes.

2 cups confectioners' sugar

4 tablespoons unsalted butter, at room temperature

4 tablespoons heavy (whipping) cream

1 teaspoon vanilla extract

¼ teaspoon salt

1 tablespoon matcha powder

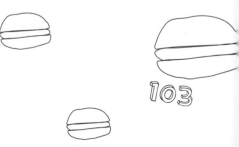

103

What is matcha?

Matcha powder is a finely ground green tea used to lend a
mild, herbal flavor and a bright green hue to baked goods,
ice creams, and noodles. Matcha has also garnered a great
deal of attention for its antibiotic and antioxidant properties;
however, the whoopie pie application has zero health benefits.
Its emerald color is just so pretty!

vegan chocolate "butter" cream

In the work bowl of a stand mixer fitted with the paddle attachment, beat together the butter substitute, sugar, cocoa powder, rice milk, and vanilla on low until just combined. Increase the speed to medium and beat until smooth and creamy, about 3 minutes.

Note: If you can find it, try coconut oil as the non-dairy butter substitute. It will intensify the flavor of your vegan fillings.

3 tablespoons non-dairy butter substitute, preferably Smart Balance Buttery Spread

1⅓ cups confectioners' sugar

⅓ cup cocoa powder

¼ cup rice milk

1 teaspoon vanilla extract

105

Vegan Vanilla "butter" cream

8 tablespoons non-dairy butter substitute, preferably Smart Balance Buttery Spread

8 ounces non-dairy cream cheese substitute, preferably Tofutti Better Than Cream Cheese

3 tablespoons non-dairy sour cream substitute, preferably Tofutti Better Than Sour Cream

3 cups confectioners' sugar

1 teaspoon vanilla extract

In the work bowl of a stand mixer fitted with the paddle attachment, beat together the butter substitute and Tofutti cream cheese and sour cream on medium speed until combined. Add the sugar and vanilla and beat on low until just combined. Increase the speed to medium and beat until smooth and creamy, about 3 minutes.

bacon-chive goat cheese

In a medium skillet, cook the bacon over medium heat until crisp. Using a slotted spoon, transfer the bacon to a paper-towel-lined plate to drain and cool. When cool, crumble into small pieces.

In the work bowl of a stand mixer fitted with the paddle attachment, beat together the goat cheese, cream cheese, and milk on low speed until just combined. Increase the speed to medium and beat until smooth and creamy, about 3 minutes. Add the crumbled bacon and the chives and beat on low until combined.

6 slices bacon

4 ounces soft fresh goat cheese, at room temperature

4 ounces cream cheese, at room temperature

2 tablespoons milk

1 tablespoon chopped fresh chives

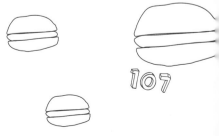

107

chocolate glaze

1½ cups (8 ounces) semisweet or bittersweet chocolate chips

1 cup heavy (whipping) cream

1 tablespoon unsalted butter, at room temperature

Put the chocolate in a heatproof bowl. Heat the cream in a small, heavy saucepan over medium heat just until it bubbles. Pour the hot cream over the chocolate in the bowl and stir with a wooden spoon until smooth. Add the butter and stir to blend. Use immediately.

Note: For a smooth, even glaze, dip your assembled whoopie pies into the warm glaze, then cool on a rack. Place a sheet of parchment or waxed paper under the rack to catch the drippings.

ingredients & sources

ingredients

Coconut Oil

We like Spectrum Organic coconut oils; the refined or unrefined versions are equally good. You can find them at Whole Foods and other fine grocery stores.

www.spectrumorganics.com

Freeze-Dried Fruits

Delicious freeze-dried fruits—including strawberries, peaches, apples, and bananas—are perfect for mixing into whoopie pie fillings.

www.justtomatoes.com

Marshmallow Fluff

The original marshmallow cream, perfect for whoopie pie filling.

www.marshmallowfluff.com

Matcha Powder

You can buy matcha powder that is specifically blended for various uses, including baking, cocktails, frozen desserts, or smoothies, at Teanobi, a San Francisco specialty tea company.

www.teanobi.com

sources

BevMo

If it is legal to ship alcohol to your state (not in Pennsylvania, kiddies), BevMo stocks root beer Schnapps (a killer addition not only to whoopie pie cake batter and creamy fillings, but also to an adult root beer float).

www.bevmo.com

Bob's Red Mill

Bob's Red Mill Natural Foods has more than 400 products for baking, including top-quality oats and a line of gluten-free flours, baking mixes, and grains.

www.bobsredmill.com

Crate and Barrel

This kitchenware and home furnishings store carries bakeware large and small.
www.crateandbarrel.com

Kalustyan's

Kalustyan's sells a wide range of spices, oils, candied/dried fruits, and flavorings, such as rose essence and rosewater.

www.kalustyans.com

King Arthur Flour

King Arthur is a fantastic source for bakeware, tools, mixes, flour, and flavorings, as well as sanding sugars, nonpareils, and other decorative elements. You can find rosewater, nut flavors, lime powder, and all sorts of other inspiring flavors to experiment with in your baking.

www.kingarthurflour.com

Sur la Table

You'll find kitchen- and bakeware galore here, including baking sheets, Silpats, and parchment paper.

www.surlatable.com

Williams-Sonoma

Williams-Sonoma sells bakeware, stand mixers, and a multitude of kitchen tools, including Silpats and two-tablespoon measuring spoons.

www.williams-sonoma.com

Wilton

Wilton sells anything you can imagine for baking and cake decorating, including pastry tips and bags and food colorings.

www.wilton.com

Zatarains

Zatarains sells a full range of Cajun products, including spices, rice blends, and root beer extract.

www.zatarains.com

where to find a whoopie pie near you

Amish Door Village

1210 Winesburg Street
US 62
Wilmot, OH 44689
888-264-7436

www.amishdoormarketplace.com

Bird-in-Hand Bakehouse

542 Gibbons Road
Bird-in-Hand, PA 17505
717-656-7947

www.bihbakeshop.com

Cranberry Island Kitchen

7B Corey Road
Cumberland, ME 04021
207-829-5200

www.cranberryislandkitchen.com

Gobba Gobba Hey

This food cart is found on the streets of the Mission District of San Francisco, CA.

www.gobbagobbahey.com

Isamax Snacks

1 Commonwealth Avenue
Gardiner, ME 04345
877-447-2629

www.wickedwhoopies.com

One Girl Cookies

68 Dean Street
Brooklyn, NY 11201
212-675-4996

www.onegirlcookies.com

Steve's Snacks

9 Jewett Street
Skowhegan, ME 04976
207-858-0139

www.stevessnacks.com

West Coast Whoopies

1007 Calimesa Boulevard
Calimesa, CA 92320
909-795-8788

www.westcoastwhoopies.com

WhoopiePies.com

20 Haley Street
Lewiston, ME 04240
207-240-9350

www.whoopiepies.com

Urban Rustic

236 N. 12th Street
Brooklyn, NY 11211
718-388-9444

www.urbanrusticnyc.com

Zingerman's Bakehouse

3711 Plaza Drive
Ann Arbor, MI 48108
734-761-2095

www.zingermansbakehouse.com

festival

Whoopie Pie Festival
Held annually
Hershey Farm Restaurant & Inn
Route 896
Strasburg, PA 17572
717-687-8635

www.whoopiepiefestival.com

photo credits

PAGE 2
Just baked Classic
Chocolate Whoopie
(43)

PAGE 28–29
The Purist.
Classic Chocolate Whoopie (43) with
Classic Marshmallow filling (76),
decorated with multicolored sprinkles

PAGE 34–35
The Purist.
Classic Chocolate Whoopie (43) with
Classic Marshmallow filling (76),
decorated with multicolored sprinkles

PAGE 38
Classic Chocolate
Whoopie (43) cooling
on rack

PAGE 40
Piping Classic Marsh-
mallow filling (76)
onto Classic Chocolate
Whoopie (43)

PAGE 42
Classic Chocolate
Whoopie (43) with
Classic Marshmallow
filling (76)

PAGE 45
Red Velvet Whoopie (44)
with Classic Marshmallow
filling (76)

PAGE 47
Vanilla Whoopie (46)
with Chocolate Butter-
cream filling (79)

PAGE 51
Chocolate Chip
Whoopie (50) with
Classic Marshmallow
filling (76)

PAGE 56
Rock the Casbah.
Pistachio-Cardamom
Whoopie (57) with
Rosewater Buttercream
filling (86)

PAGE 59
S'mores Whoopie.
Graham Cracker
Whoopie (58) with
Chocolate Ganache
(82) and Classic
Marshmallow
filling (76)

PAGE 60
Brisk Morning Constitutional.
Oatmeal Whoopie (61) with
Maple-Bacon filling (94)

PAGE 63
Pumpkin Whoopie (62)
with Classic Cream
Cheese filling (80)

PAGE 70
Whoopie Cake.
Classic Chocolate
Whoopie (43) with Classic
Marshmallow filling (76)

PAGE 72
Jalapeño Cornbread
Whoopie (73) with
Bacon-Chive Goat
Cheese filling (107)

PAGE 77
The Candy Striper.
Classic Chocolate Whoopie
(43) with Mint Buttercream
filling (84) decorated with
crushed peppermint candies

PAGE 78
Mexican Chocolate.
Classic Chocolate Whoopie
(43) with spiced Chocolate
Ganache filling (82) decorated
with crushed cocoa nibs

PAGE 102
Classic Chocolate
Whoopie (43) with
Matcha Buttercream
filling (103)

PAGE 109
Black & White.
Classic Chocolate Whoopie
(43) and Vanilla Whoopie
(46) with Classic Marsh-
mallow filling (76) dipped
in Chocolate Glaze (108)

PAGE 110
The Purist.
Classic Chocolate Whoopie
(43) with Classic Marsh-
mallow filling (76), decorated with multicolored
sprinkles

table of equivalents

The exact equivalents in the following tables have been rounded for convenience.

Liquid/Dry Measurements

U.S.	Metric
¼ teaspoon	1.25 milliliters
½ teaspoon	2.5 milliliters
1 teaspoon	5 milliliters
1 tablespoon (3 teaspoons)	15 milliliters
1 fluid ounce (2 tablespoons)	30 milliliters
¼ cup	60 milliliters
⅓ cup	80 milliliters
½ cup	120 milliliters
1 cup	240 milliliters
1 pint (2 cups)	480 milliliters
1 quart (4 cups, 32 ounces)	960 milliliters
1 gallon (4 quarts)	3.84 liters
1 ounce (by weight)	28 grams
1 pound	448 grams
2.2 pounds	1 kilogram

Lengths

U.S.	Metric
⅛ inch	3 millimeters
¼ inch	6 millimeters
½ inch	12 millimeters
1 inch	2.5 centimeters

Oven Temperature

Fahrenheit	Celsius	Gas
250	120	½
275	140	1
300	150	2
325	160	3
350	180	4
375	190	5
400	200	6
425	220	7
450	230	8
475	240	9
500	260	10

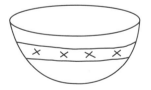

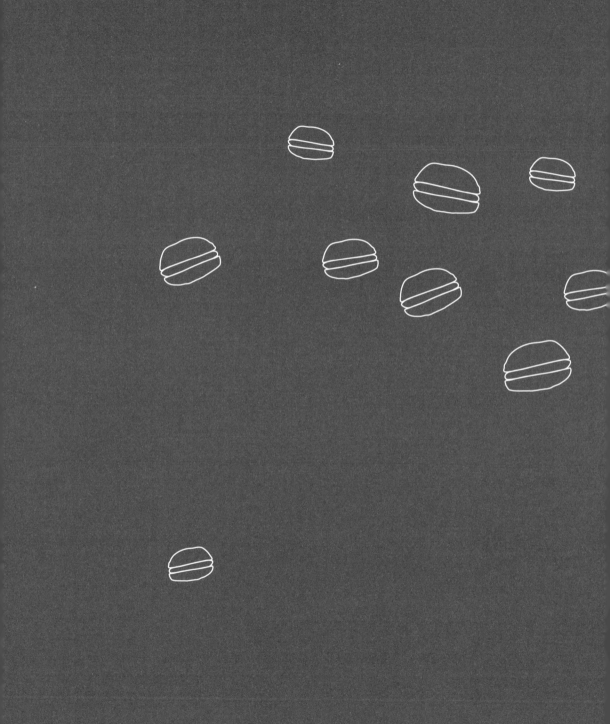